Proofs of the Existence of the Soul

By
Annie Besant

ISBN: 978-1-63118-638-7

Esoteric Classics

Other Books in this Series and Related Titles

Hypnotism and Mesmerism by Annie Besant (978–1–63118–587–8)

The Hidden Language of Symbolism by Annie Besant (978–1–63118–585–4)

Memory and Consciousness by Besant & Blavatsky (978–1–63118–582–3)

Occultism, Semi-Occultism & Pseudo Occultism by A Besant (978–1–63118–577–9)

Spiritual Life for Man by Annie Besant (978–1–63118–573–1)

The Mysteries by Annie Besant (978–1–63118–572–4)

Communication Between Different Worlds by Annie Besant (978–1–63118–569–4)

The Brotherhood of Religions by Annie Besant (978–1–63118–563–2)

Clairvoyance and Psychic Abilities by A Besant &c (978-1-63118-403-1)

Spiritual Progress and Practical Occultism by H P Blavatsky (978–1–63118–583–0)

Alchemy in the Nineteenth Century by Helena P. Blavatsky (978-1-63118-446-8)

Rosicrucians and Speculative Masonry in the Seventeenth Century (978-1-63118-489-5)

Qabbalistic Teachings and the Tree of Life by M P Hall (978-1-63118-482-6)

Early Masonic Symbolism by Manly P Hall (978–1–63118–606–6)

Fortune-Telling with Dice by Astra Cielo (978-1-63118-466-6)

History, Analysis and Secret Tradition of the Tarot by Hall &c (978-1-63118-445-1)

Crystal Vision Through Crystal Gazing by Frater Achad (978-1-63118-455-0)

Arcane Formulas or Mental Alchemy by W W Atkinson (978-1-63118-459-8)

The Machinery of the Mind by Dion Fortune (978-1-63118-451-2)

The A E Waite Reader: A Selection of Occult Essays (978-1-63118-515-1)

The Leadbeater Reader: A Selection of Occult Essays (978-1-63118-483-3)

Audio versions are also available on Audible, Amazon and Apple

Other Books in this Series and Related Titles

Mysteries of the Sacraments by Annie Besant (978-1-63118-636-3)

Spiritualism and Theosophy by Henry S. Olcott (978-1-63118-629-5)

Duties of a Theosophist by Annie Besant (978-1-63118-628-8)

The Book of the Nephilim by Enoch (978-1-63118-627-1)

Building Occult Character by Besant & Leadbeater (978-1-63118-626-4)

Ancient Egyptian Mysteries and Hieroglyphics, Modern Freemasonry & Initiation of the Pyramid (978-1-63118-625-7) HC

The Lost Book of Noah by Noah (978-1-63118-624-0)

The Acts of Saint Andrew by Andrew (978-1-63118-623-3)

The Acts of the Apostle John by John (978–1–63118–622–6)

Karmic Visions by Helena P. Blavatsky (978–1–63118–621–9)

The Ascension of Isaiah by Isaiah (978-1-63118-620-2)

The Mysteries of Mithra by G R S Mead (978-1-63118-619-6)

Second Book of Enoch by Enoch (978-1-63118-617-2)

Lost Keys of Freemasonry by Manly P Hall (978-1-63118-616-5)

Book of the Watchers by Enoch (978-1-63118-615-8)

Sepher Yetzirah and the Qabalah by Manly P Hall (978-1-63118-614-1)

Philosophy of Self-Knowledge by Franz Hartmann (978-1-63118-613-4)

Occult Symbolism of the Sun and Moon, the Goddess Isis and thee Solar Deities by Manly P Hall (978–1–63118–611–0)

Practical Theosophy by Annie Besant (978–1–63118–610–3)

The Human Body in Symbolism by Manly P Hall (978–1–63118–609–7)

Audio versions are also available on Audible, Amazon and Apple

Table of Contents

INTRODUCTION

The word "esoteric" can be difficult to define. Esotericism in general can be seen less as a system of beliefs and more as a category, which encompasses numerous, different systems of beliefs. It's a bit of juxtaposition, since the word "esoteric" indicates something that few people know about, while the term itself broadly covers numerous philosophies, practices, areas of study and belief systems.

In a greater sense, Esotericism acts as a storehouse for secret knowledge, which is often considered ancient *(by tradition, if not by fact),* passed down from generation to generation, in private. At various times in history, simply possessing the knowledge of some of these subjects, was considered illegal and a jailable offence, if discovered. This usually included such general topics as Alchemy, Pharmacology, Qabalah, Hermeticism, Occultism, Ceremonial Magic, Astrology, Divination, Rosicrucianism and so on. Collectively, these areas of study were often referred to as the esoteric sciences.

Sometimes, the outer garment of a subject isn't esoteric, while what is hidden beneath it, is. As an example, Freemasonry isn't necessarily esoteric by nature *(at least not anymore),* but certain signs, passwords and handshakes given to the candidate during their initiation, are in fact, esoteric, in the sense that they are hidden from the general public.

Today, in the twenty-first century, such topics are readily available at bookstores across the country, and numerous main-steam publishers offer beginners guides and coffee-table volumes on many of these subjects, intended for mass appeal. Books like "*The Secret*" have turned previously arcane topics into household knowledge. All that being the case, however, it isn't to say that there still aren't buried secrets to uncover, ancient wisdom being ignored and forgotten mysteries to be explored. In fact, it is often that we are only able to further our own studies by standing on the shoulders of these disappearing giants.

Lamp of Trismegistus is doing its part to help preserve humanity's esoteric history by making some of these classics available to those students who are seeking to unearth the knowledge of these ancient colossi.

So, be sure to check other titles from our *Esoteric Classics* series, as well as our *Occult Fiction*, *Theosophical Classics*, *Foundations of Freemasonry Series*, *Studies in Alchemy*, *Supernatural Fiction*, *Paranormal Research Series*, *Studies in Buddhism* and our *Christian Apocrypha Series.* You can also download the audio versions of most of these titles from Amazon, Apple or Audible, for learning on the go.

ANNIE BESANT:
A LUMINARY OF THEOSOPHY AND ESOTERICISM

Annie Besant, a significant figure in the spiritual milieu of the 19th and 20th centuries, represents a unique blend of activism, education, and spiritual exploration. She is perhaps best known for her pivotal role in the Theosophical Society, which was committed to studying comparative religion, philosophy, and science, and promoting the universal brotherhood of humanity. However, Besant's interest in and contributions to Theosophy and the occult, as well as her other esoteric connections, provide a deeper understanding of her life and work.

Born on October 1, 1847, in London, Besant's early life was deeply influenced by a rigorous religious education, which spurred a lifelong quest for spiritual and philosophical truth. However, it wasn't until her introduction to the works of Helena Petrovna Blavatsky, the co-founder of the Theosophical Society with Henry S. Olcott, that Besant found a framework that resonated deeply with her own esoteric leanings.

Joining the Theosophical Society in 1889 marked a turning point in Besant's life. Her keen intellect and voracious curiosity made her a natural fit for the society, and she soon emerged as a leading figure within the organization; in fact, Besant's encounters with Blavatsky and Olcott led to profound transformations in her personal and intellectual life and played a crucial role in shaping her future as a theosophist.

Besant's initial introduction to theosophy was through her encounters with Blavatsky's writings. The book "The Secret Doctrine," Blavatsky's magnum opus, was particularly influential. The text's exploration of the synthesis of science, religion, and philosophy intrigued Besant, sparking a desire to explore these concepts further. Besant was deeply moved by the central tenets of theosophy – universal brotherhood, the study of comparative religion, philosophy, and science, and the investigation of the unexplained laws of nature and the powers latent in humanity.

Intrigued by these ideas, Besant met with Blavatsky in 1889, marking the beginning of a relationship that would significantly shape her spiritual path. Blavatsky recognized Besant's potential and quickly became her mentor, guiding her into the theosophical fold. Besant, impressed by Blavatsky's intellect and spiritual insight, described her as a "great teacher" and a "friend."

Under Blavatsky's guidance, Besant rapidly advanced within the Theosophical Society, with her intellect and passion making her a natural fit for leadership roles. When Blavatsky died in 1891, Besant was among the members who were instrumental in carrying forward her legacy.

Besant's relationship with Henry Steel Olcott, the co-founder and first President of the Theosophical Society, was decidedly different but also played a significant role in her involvement with theosophy. Although Olcott was primarily based in Asia, his correspondence and occasional meetings with Besant helped deepen her understanding of theosophy and its objectives. Olcott's emphasis on practical spirituality and service, as well as his efforts to reconcile Western and Eastern spiritual traditions, deeply resonated with Besant. His influence would be seen in her later work in India, where she embraced and promoted Hindu philosophy and culture, just as Olcott had done with Buddhism in Sri Lanka.

After Olcott's death in 1907, Besant became President of the Theosophical Society, a position she held until her death in 1933. In this role, she was able to build upon the foundations laid by Blavatsky and Olcott, expanding the reach of theosophy and promoting its principles worldwide.

The relationships with Blavatsky and Olcott had a profound influence on Besant's life and work. They marked the beginning of her journey into theosophy and the esoteric, offering guidance, inspiration, and a platform for her to explore and share her spiritual insights. This trilateral bond between Besant, Blavatsky, and Olcott became a cornerstone of theosophical history, shaping not just Besant's personal journey, but also the broader trajectory of the Theosophical Society.

Besant's overall involvement in Theosophy was marked by a deep commitment to the exploration of the esoteric and the occult. She authored numerous works on these subjects, including "The Ancient Wisdom" and "Thought Power: Its Control and Culture", contributing significantly to the society's body of knowledge. These works delved into various aspects of metaphysics, spirituality, and the occult, offering comprehensive insights into the esoteric wisdom that lay at the heart of theosophy.

Throughout her tenure as leader of the Theosophical Society, Besant demonstrated a profound interest in eastern religions, particularly Hinduism and Buddhism. She believed that these ancient wisdom traditions held key insights into the nature of reality and the human spirit. Besant's efforts helped to bridge the gap between Eastern and Western spiritual thought, fostering a greater understanding and appreciation of these traditions among Western audiences.

Beyond her work in Theosophy, Besant's interests extended to various other esoteric fields. She studied and wrote about astrology, alchemy, and mysticism, drawing connections between these disciplines and theosophical thought. She also explored the realms of psychic phenomena and spiritualism, contributing to a growing body of literature on these subjects at the time.

Besant's influence extended well beyond the confines of the Theosophical Society. In India, she was deeply involved in the nation's struggle for independence, and she also contributed to the field of education by establishing the Central Hindu College in Benares, which later became a part of the Banaras Hindu University.

Annie Besant's life and work represent a remarkable fusion of spiritual exploration, esoteric scholarship, and activism. Her significant contributions to Theosophy, her insights into the occult, and her commitment to bridging the gap between Eastern and Western spiritual traditions mark her as a leading figure in the history of esoteric thought. Even today, her writings continue to inspire and guide those who venture into the realm of the spiritual and the esoteric.

PROOFS OF THE EXISTENCE OF THE SOUL

In all ages of the world, among all civilizations and all peoples, there has existed that ineradicable assurance in man which we find expressed in the words of a Roman: *Not all of me shall die.* But that conviction is not in the ordinary sense of the word in itself a proof. It might be argued from, as found everywhere and at all times, as apparently being part of human nature; but when I use the word "proof or proofs of the existence of the soul", I do not mean to appeal to that intuition, nor to base my argument on that often-expressed conviction.

I intend to try to lead you step by step along a line of thought upon which the materialist might begin, although he would lose his materialism ere advancing very far; and I want to show you that in dealing with the soul we can proceed from step to step by clear and logical argument, so that the most reasonable and logical of people may be led gradually to admit the existence of a soul; or, at least, we can carry them at first to this point, that the balance of argument is in favor of such an existence, and that undoubtedly something exists beyond the brain. What that something is, is to be investigated by a different method of study. And this is much, when we can take a materialist and show him that a line of thought and of experiment is open to him which will land him in a position which almost compels him to advance, places him at a point where he can hardly logically stop, and so makes at least a *prima facie* ground which he may take as a platform from which to go further, as offering a sufficiently reasonable hypothesis to encourage a still deeper investigation.

Let us for a moment consider the basis of the materialistic argument with regard to thought and brain. It is an argument that now is falling entirely out of scientific favor, but it held a very high ground among scientific men some five-and-twenty years ago; and at that time you could take up writer after writer amongst the respected scientists of the world, and you would be led by the whole tenor of their argument to conclude that, although they did not say so in so many words, thought was really the production, the result, of matter. Professor Tyndall in that famous Belfast address, when he was dealing with matter and mind, said, as you may remember, that science would probably have entirely to recast its conceptions of matter; and that is most certainly a true prophecy. Since the Belfast address was delivered, science *has* changed its conception of matter. It no longer gives to it the very narrow definition that it used to give in the days, say, of the youth of many of us. We find that nowadays matter is recognized as existing under conditions that five-and-twenty years ago would have been regarded as excluding the word *material,* or as making it inapplicable.

Now, the old argument used to run, if I may just hastily go over it — for it was very familiar to me in the earlier days of my own thinking — that thought was directly produced by the action of the grey matter of the brain; that wherever such matter was found, thought was found in connection with it; that wherever it was not found, thought was absent; and that it was even possible to trace a quantitative relation between the amount of grey matter and the power of the thought. Not only was this put in a general way, but it was worked out with extreme care. You remember the old line along which the development of thought was traced in the growing child; how it was said that if you took a child's brain, the thought it could produce was infantile in its character; that as the brain developed into boyhood, thought grew stronger; that as the boy grew into a man, thought grew more powerful, more subtle; that as the man reached maturity the thought ripened with the growing maturity of the man; that if at any stage of that man's life the brain was injured, then the thought was changed in its character; that if the supply of blood were injured, say as by any intoxicating liquor, then thought became confused with the confused state of the brain; that if you found fever, so that the blood was in a bad condition, you had delirium affecting the thought; that if a bit of the skull-pan pressed on the brain, at once thought was entirely either changed or disappeared, whereas, when you again lifted that piece of broken bone, thought returned. As the man grew old, thought weakened. When the brain began to decay, thought entirely vanished. If one little piece of the brain was eaten away, the faculty of the mind that expressed itself through that part of the brain disappeared. And then the argument was triumphantly summed up. If thought grows and increases and ripens with the growth and the increase and the ripening of the brain, if it varies with brain conditions, if it vanishes when the brain is seriously injured, if it grows weaker with the weakening of the brain, if as the brain decays thought-power disappears, can we venture to say that when the brain falls to pieces after death, thought rises triumphant from its ruins and exists in strength and in majesty?

And the argument was a very strong argument, exceedingly strong to anyone who was accustomed to reason from point to point and to follow wherever the process of reasoning led. But the whole of that argument was based on induction. A conclusion can be reached by inductive logic, but there is always one difficulty in connection with any such argument. You must be sure that in any induction the whole of the facts are before you, for one fact omitted from your basis vitiates the whole of your conclusion. If one thing is left out, the whole superstructure falls; and always the weakness of the inductive argument is the possibility of some one fact having been overlooked. Unless you are sure that you know everything in the universe of discourse, inductive logic does not lead you to a certain and final conclusion.

Now, it was by the discovery of facts which were not included in that famous inductive argument, that the whole superstructure fell to pieces. One fact alone would have been enough, but instead of one, hundreds have come to the front. In any argument which is based on the constant relation between two things, that constant relation must be shown to exist; and if you can get those same two things moving in an opposite direction, varying inversely, then what becomes of your argument? Now that is exactly what has happened in connection with the argument based on brain and thought and their constantly varying together. It has been found that they do not constantly vary together, and still more that they sometimes vary inversely; that is, that you may get a condition where the brain is partially paralyzed, but where the thought is very much more active than when it was working in the brain.

Now, in these first steps of my argument I am not going to prove the soul, but I am going to prove that consciousness may exist apart from a physical organism; for it is that which needs to be proved first before a materialist will listen to you at all. There is no good talking about the soul as long as any person is of the opinion that thought is only the product of the brain — to use Carl Vogt's expression — as bile is the product of the liver. So long as a person holds that position, as some people do, you must shake him out of it by facts that he will recognize before you can begin to talk about the soul; and as every one agrees that the soul is connected with consciousness, if we can show that consciousness exists apart from that constant relation between brain and thought, we shall have made our first step out of materialism, and then we shall feel free to go further on in tracing the nature of this consciousness.

Now, speaking generally, a mass of mesmeric and hypnotic experiments put it beyond the possibility of challenge that intelligence can work when the brain is paralyzed.

I prefer in dealing with this question not to take experiments which rest on the evidence of those who might be regarded as people to be challenged, because they are looked on more or less as *cranks,* like Theosophists. I had rather take some good scientific man, a materialist, to begin with, because his evidence is so much more satisfactory to his fellow-materialists. Always, if you can, get your opponent to prove your case; to prove your own case out of the mouth of your opponent's witness is supposed to be a triumph, I understand, in legal procedure. I shall therefore summon, into my witness-box some of the doctors in Paris who are materialists — they call themselves so; I am not calling them names — but who are utterly unable to account for the results that they have themselves obtained. Quite honestly they say that they do not put forward a theory; they simply record the facts that they have observed — a perfectly sound and proper position and a very useful one to take up.

Now, amongst their observations — for I have no time to dwell on them long — we find this: they have invented an apparatus which tests the physical condition of the beating of the heart while the patient is in the hypnotic state. They have some admirable instruments by which they can measure exactly the beating of the heart, the movement of the lungs, the contraction of the muscles, and so on. So that by means of this apparatus they can get a perfectly accurate record of the physical conditions of the person under observation, a quite necessary thing when you want to proceed slowly from step to step. The instrument that they generally use is one in which a revolving cylinder, covered with black-lead paper, is set going, with a pencil attached to some part of the patient's body, according to the nature of the observation — attached to a lever, and the lever in turn attached to the body, so that any motion in that part of the patient's body is reproduced by the pencil pressing against the cylinder; as the cylinder revolves the pencil would draw a straight line if there were no motion, but any motion will produce a curve.

Now, suppose you had such a machine attached to your heart, you would get then a series of curves traced on this black-lead paper showing the beating of the heart, and the slightest irregularity in the heart would at once be marked in a very magnified form in the curves traced by the pencil on this cylinder. So again with any movement of the lungs. There is a definite movement of the lungs and the curve would be recognized by any doctor. So again, if you are dealing with muscular contractions. If you stretch out your arm straight, and you have a weight in the hand, there is action taking place in the muscle — vibrations — and that increases tremendously in activity as the arm is held out longer and longer, the effort increasing with the time of the extension of the muscle.

Now, all these precautions are taken in order to eliminate every possibility of fraud or cheating, so as to get an absolutely accurate physical record of the state of the patient's body; and they have thus shown that when a person is in a hypnotic trance the beating of the heart is entirely changed, and finally reaches a point so slight that although the movement is still shown on the revolving cylinder, no instrument less delicate would show it was beating at all. The same with the lungs; the movement of the lungs is so slight that no breath can be found coming from the lips. So also in regard to muscles. There is a distinct trace which enables them to say whether or not the man, with the outstretched arm heavily weighted, is or is not in a hypnotic state.

Now, what is the condition of the brain when the body is like that? In the first place the blood-supply is checked. The blood moves very sluggishly through the vessels of the brain and in the tiny vessels, the capillary vessels, its movement is stopped. Not only is the supply of blood in this way entirely changed in its motion, but the blood is very bad of its kind, for as it is not properly aired in travelling through the lungs, it is very much overcharged with all the products of decomposition, and you have quantities of carbonic acid. The result of that is very well known. It brings about a state of coma, a state in which no thought is possible, so far as the brain is concerned. So that we get a person who cannot think with the brain. The brain is stopped. It is placed in a state in which anyone, twenty-five years ago, would have said thought is impossible. You have brought about a physical condition in which thought must vanish; and so it does, so far as that physical body is concerned. The creature lies there as though he were dead; but you are able to reach him without altering these physical conditions; you are able to obtain from him mental results, and when a person is in that state you can show that his mental faculties are immensely stimulated, that his memory has quite changed its character; that he can tell you incidents of his childhood which in his normal state had quite passed from him; that he will sometimes speak a language which he heard as a tiny child and has since entirely forgotten, so that if it is spoken in his presence he is not able to understand it. You will find that the memory is so intensified in its immediate action, leaving the past out of sight, that if you take up a Greek book and the man is ignorant of Greek, and you read over a page from that book, he will repeat it word for word without a blunder. Wake him up and he cannot say it, cannot pronounce a single syllable. Throw him back into the hypnotic state, and he will repeat it over again and again. Not only have you thus a very different kind of memory, but you also can obtain a far higher grade of intelligence. A person who is stupid in his waking consciousness is often clever when he is under hypnotic control; not that he reproduces the thought of the hypnotizer, as indeed he will do if he is made to, but he will dwell on things where the hypnotizer is thinking on other lines, and will argue with him. Cases are on record where a man abnormally stupid has shown acuteness in his argument when he is in a state in which the brain cannot work. And so over and over again you get placed on record these observations of abnormal knowledge, manifested when the brain is rendered incapable of sane and healthy thought.

The next thing that you remark in dealing with such a person is that you can entirely deceive the senses, and make them give reports which are absolutely erroneous; that you can make him see what is not visible; and you can equally easily make him not see what is visible; that, for instance, you can make yourself invisible, and if you like you can leave yourself tangible but invisible, so that he may walk right up against you as though you were not there, and start when, coming against you, he finds an obstacle that he cannot see. So you can alter the sense of hearing; you can make him hear or not hear, as you please. So you can, if you like, destroy the sense of touch so that he shall not feel, or you can do the opposite and you can make him feel a solid body by simply stating that it lies between his hands. You can make him smell a sweet odor when you present to him some repulsive article. You can play with the senses as you can stimulate the mind. You can prove still more than this by taking an ordinary person and thus hypnotizing him.

I now pass from the Paris hospitals to statements made by doctors in care of the insane asylums. If you take an ordinary lunatic and throw him into the hypnotic state, you can obtain from him in some cases intelligence and reasoning power. The moment he is out of that condition he is again a lunatic, but under hypnotism he becomes an intelligent thinker.

Now, these things are done over and over again. Suppose you prove that instead of thought varying with the state of the brain it varies against it; that when the brain is in a state of coma, thought is exceptionally active; that when the brain is paralyzed, memory is exceptionally acute and brings back events that are long forgotten; what is the inevitable inference? That although thought may continually be expressed through the brain, it is also possible to express it without the brain; that although it is true that many events remain in the normal memory and others are forgotten, those forgotten events are not really forgotten; they remain in consciousness, although out of sight; they can be brought up by consciousness, although normally they have vanished. So that you are led inevitably by these observations, which can be repeated indefinitely, to realize that human consciousness is something more than is expressed through the physical brain.

I am not going to press the argument one bit beyond that, for the moment, but you can prove to demonstration that there is more consciousness in a man than comes out in his waking moments when the brain is in its normal state of activity; that he has a consciousness wider than the waking; that under abnormal conditions this consciousness emerges; that it contains the record of events that the waking consciousness has forgotten; that it is able to exercise powers keener and subtler than the powers of the waking consciousness. So that you finally come to the conclusion that whatever human consciousness may be — and on that at present we will not dogmatize — that whatever human consciousness may be, it is something more than that which we know in our healthy waking moments, and that there is more of us than is expressed through the brain, that we are able to produce more in consciousness than our brain allows us to express; and so we arrive at the rather startling conclusion that the brain is a limitation placed on our consciousness; a partial instrument, instead of the producer, of thought.

That is, we have entirely reversed the materialistic position. Instead of the brain producing thought, thought expresses itself partially through the brain. As much of it as can get through comes through, and the rest remains for the time unexpressed but not non-existent. This is so much recognized now that all these French schools will divide consciousness, and tell you about the waking consciousness and the dream consciousness, that which is called the subliminal consciousness. There are all sorts of wonderful terms, which I sometimes think do more to cover ignorance than to express knowledge, and we constantly find the most wonderfully complicated expressions which are intended to convey the idea that I have put into rather rough phrase, that there is more of us in consciousness than comes through the brain.

Now, all these discoveries have very much intensified scientific investigation along the lines of this consciousness which does not work in the physical brain; and you have men like James Sully, men like Sidgwick, who are leading English writers on psychology, giving a very large part of their time to the state of the consciousness which is outside the waking. Why, some years ago, if people had studied dreams, they would have been thought as foolish as Theosophists are thought now; but today the study of dreams is highly scientific. You need not be the least afraid of losing your character as sane and rational people by the study of dreams. On the contrary, you will only be advanced people, going along the lines of the most advanced science, rather, in fact, beyond your neighbors than below them in intelligence; and this has been the result of finding out how much is to be learned by studies of the dream state; and that is our next step.

Now, there have been certain very interesting-physiological measurements made, and if science is good at anything it is good at measuring. It is extraordinary the way modern science measures, the accuracy, the delicacy of it, the way in which by its balances it will weigh, I am afraid to say how tiny a fraction of a grain; and there is nothing in which science has made more remarkable advance than in the exquisite delicacy of its instruments whereby it measures what would seem immeasurably minute results. And another thing that is admirable is the wonderful patience of these scientific investigators. Clifford once spoke of the sublime patience of the investigator; and the term is not misapplied. Their patience really is sublime. They will do the same minute experiment over a hundred, or two or three hundred, times in order to be sure that they are right; and I hold that to be a most admirable quality, both mentally and morally; morally, because it implies that love of the truth which will take unending pains before it will make an assertion or accept the record of a fact; and I say this all the more strongly because it is sometimes thought that Theosophy is against science. That is not so. We give the fullest admiration and homage to the patience and the care, the reverence for truth, shown by the modern scientific men. All we object to is when they make inferences too hastily, and then assert their inferences as definitely as they assert their facts. Then we get rather into quarrels sometimes with them, because we cannot take all the inferences they make, knowing as we do that the inferences are based on incomplete knowledge of the facts.

Now, one of the things that science has been measuring is the rate of the nervous wave in the physical organization — how long it takes for a wave to pass along nervous matter, to be transmitted from cells to cells — a fairly difficult thing to observe, I mean with the accuracy with which it has been done; but some of our German friends, especially, who are nothing if they are not accurate, have gone very carefully into these measurements. They have found out the fraction of a second which it takes for a wave or vibration in nervous matter to occur, so that they are able to tell us exactly just how long it takes for such a wave of nervous motion to travel, and that means how many such waves can occur in any given track of nerve within a second of time. They can tell how many such vibrations can be received in a second. Let us suppose for the moment — for the number does not matter for our purpose — let us suppose that they found that nervous matter could receive a hundred vibrations per second. You know that the nervous matter of the eye, for instance, if it receives vibrations within less than one-tenth of a second, yields a continuous impression. If your impressions come at more than that rate you get then a continuous line. If you get an impression separated from others by more than one-tenth of a second, you see that impression by itself. Now apply that to the states of consciousness of the later investigations, and you find that a certain number of impressions can be made on the nerve, representing states of consciousness, or succession of thoughts. Let us suppose that a hundred of these can take place in one second. Now go to sleep and dream, and within one second of physical time you may have thoughts experienced by the intelligence at the comparative rate of four or five thousand or more in the second. You may live in the dream consciousness through a year, and every event may be there; you may go through them; one after another; day after day, and night after night, you may experience successive events, you may live through troubles and joys; all these intellectual results may be experienced, and when you are awaked one second of physical time only has passed, and yet you have gone through states of consciousness that the nervous system would demand a year to accomplish. Nevertheless you have thought; those states of consciousness have existed; you are able to recall them, and they have gone at this immense rate; your intelligence has been working at a hundred times the normal rate. What does that mean ? It means that it has been working in a finer kind of matter. The finer the matter, the more rapid the vibrations; the finer the matter, the more vibrations can you get in that second. If you are dealing with ordinary nervous matter it moves comparatively slowly. If you are dealing with ether it moves at a tremendous rate; and if you are dealing with matter finer than ether, then inferentially the rate would be increased proportionately to the fineness of the matter in which the vibrations were set up.

If then you are able to think at a rate beyond your power of thinking in the brain, it means that your intelligence is functioning in something finer than the brain. I do not want to press it one bit further than it goes, but it does prove to demonstration that your intelligence is working in a medium finer than nervous matter. Whatever that medium is, it is very different from the nervous matter of the brain. It may be super- ethereal, as a matter of fact it is, but we are content to take up the position, that, whatever it is, it vibrates hundreds of times faster than any nervous matter can vibrate, and therefore the intelligence has some form of expression which is not an expression by the brain. This is the point to which you are led by an argument in which no flaw can be picked. It is the first time that science has given an argument, clear and definite and impregnable, which proves beyond possibility of challenge that intelligence in man does work at a rate which the brain is unable to satisfy, and therefore whatever intelligence is and does, the medium in which it is able to function is something other than brain.

Well, so far we have gone on ground that no materialist can deny. Our next step is to show that this intelligence which is not dependent on the brain, which is able to work without it, which works better without it than it does with it, more swiftly without it than it does with it, more keenly and acutely without it than it does with it — to show that that intelligence survives death. And see how carefully we are going step by step. We are not hurrying in any way; we are not rushing over it; we are only taking the next very quiet little step. We have intelligence working without the brain while the brain is still, as you may say, in touch with that intelligence possibly; and now we are going to kill our physical brain altogether, and see whether the intelligence that functioned in it during physical life can be found functioning without it after physical death. And here, of course, people who believe in immortality have put themselves at a great disadvantage with the logical materialist by making the life of the soul to begin at birth; because it is obvious that if the soul cannot manifest at birth without a body, then it seems as though it were likely that it could not get on without a body, and so death would very much paralyze its action. That is due to a lack of philosophy which has been allowed to weaken much of our religious thought; and the giving up of the reasonable philosophy of reincarnation, or pre-existence of the soul, has struck the most deadly blow at all belief in the soul's immortality. Making it dependent on the body for its manifestation, we imply its dependence on the body for its further persistence. However, leaving that point out, because it need not necessarily come into our argument, we shall get the next definite proof from the experiments of our spiritualistic brethren, or of such men as Professor Crookes, who, although he has always refused to identify himself exactly with the spiritualistic body, has yet convinced himself, by his own careful experiments, of the truth of many of their assertions. He is a very cautious man, and he does not use the word *spirit;* but he does show that intelligent entities, after they have been living in a physical body, do again function out of that body. Of course it is not necessary that the body should have perished by death, but in most of these cases, as a matter of fact, it has. If any of you will take the trouble to turn to Professor Crookes' investigations, in which he had the medium and what is called a materialization— materialized soul, it is called, but that is a very silly expression — a materialized form present under his eyes at the same time, and read them carefully, you will be obliged to admit that there is evidence there worthy of further consideration. Of course if you have not read anything of the kind nor looked into it yourself, you will probably deny the possibility off-hand, because that is one characteristic of people — that the less they know about a thing the more emphatically do they deny it. It is a great advantage to know nothing when you want to be what an English schoolboy would call *cock-sure.* I don't know whether you have the phrase over here, but it is an ordinary bit of schoolboy's slang, and it always goes hand in hand with ignorance; but I never find it in the scientific man. He is always cautious. He says: "Well, I don't believe it; I don't think your evidence is enough". He won't deny it; whereas the ignorant person will deny with a vigor proportioned to the depth of his ignorance. Now I am supposing that somebody is willing to read; does not think he knows everything in nature; does not believe that everything within the universe is within the limit of his knowledge. If a person has reached that not very advanced position, he may condescend to look into the evidence afforded by a man like Crookes. He has, for investigating materializations, invented a convenient little lamp, which lights as soon as it is opened. The reason why he used that particular kind of light was that it is very difficult to produce a materialization under the light- waves coming either from gas or electric light. It is far easier to produce it in the dark. Now, of course, many people begin to laugh the moment that is said; they say: "Oh, yes, because it is fraudulent". That is not so; an electrician cannot produce an electric spark from his machine in a very damp atmosphere; and if you said: "Oh, that is only because you want to commit fraud". he would laugh at you. So it is true that there are certain combinations of matter which do not hold together under the vibrations of ether set up by certain kinds of light. That is all the reason. It is merely that certain wave motions break up these aggregations of ethereal matter.

Now Crookes, being a chemist and an electrician, was too much instructed to take it for granted that the only reason why darkness was demanded was fraud. He thought there might be some other reason, and he invented a particular kind of lamp — some preparation of phosphorus it was — that the materialization might take place in the dark, and that then by just opening the door of his lamp, the air would touch the preparation of phosphorus, and it would burn up and give light, so that all in the room would be clearly visible. He did this, and under these conditions he was able to see the medium lying on the sofa and touch the medium with, one hand, the medium being dressed in black, while in front of him within his reach, and he allowed to touch it, there stood the materialized form in white; so that he had the two under his eyes at the same time; no curtains or dark cupboards or anything else, but the two there in full sight at the same time, and he was allowed to handle both of them together.

Now, that is evidence good enough for any reasonable person, if you can trust the accuracy and the honesty of the investigator; and I venture to say William Crookes' name is beyond all challenge for honesty, and beyond all challenge for accuracy of observation amongst scientific people, who know the kind of experiments that he has made.

Well, in addition to a number of experiments like that, he weighed some of these forms, and he made other machines which enabled him to test the force that could be exercised without any visible force being used, and so on; so that he was able to show definitely an intelligent entity able to recall the events of the past life, holding long conversations with him after death, had been passed through.

And that experience — not always with such care, to make it scientifically certain — has been repeated over and over again by thousands of spiritualists. It is foolish to deny these facts. They are on record, and if you choose may be re-verified if you are doubtful. Fraudulent occurrences have also taken place, but to deny all materializations because of these is as though you were to deny that there is any such thing as good money, because coiners circulate false coin. Such events do occur, and anyone who goes into it knows that they occur; and I say that although I do not approve of that line of investigation, although I think it dangerous and mischievous, none the less, if the person be a materialist and has been led up to the point that we reach by the study of hypnotism and by the study of dreams, he may very well then clinch, as it were, his growing convictions by getting, or much better, by himself trying some experiments along these lines. He need not go to a medium, as three or four people of the same family, sitting together, will very easily be able to convince themselves that intelligence does exist and function on the other side of death. That very simple fact can be proved over and over again, and it is not necessary to go to any professional medium; any three or four of you, who know each other as honorable men and women, may, if you choose, prove it for yourselves. I do not advise you to do this unless you are materialists. If you are, it is worth the risk for the certainty. If you are not, if already you believe in the existence of the soul, then you won't gain very much as to the nature of its existence in that way; and it is foolish to run into danger where there is no equivalent gain. But nonetheless we are led up here, step after step, to the existence of intelligent entities whom we knew in the body and may know out of the body.

Another line of investigation here, unaccompanied by danger, is based on the fact that the soul of a person connected with a living body can pass out of that body by training, and assert itself independently of the body, both as regards itself and, if it choose, as regards others.

Now I am going a step outside the line which science would recognize or which can be verified easily by anyone. I am going now into the more difficult experiments in regard to the existence of the soul. These that I have dealt with hitherto, anybody can repeat. They are the A. B C of the study. If you are materialists, begin with these and when you have gone through them you will have convinced yourself that a living intelligence can function without the assistance of the brain in or out of the physical body. You will have gone so far, and when you have reached that, you may be willing to take the trouble necessary for the more difficult experiments that follow, those which alone prove the existence of the soul, though the others prove the existence of intelligence outside the physical organism.

I am now going further. I mean by the soul a living, self-conscious intelligence, showing forth mental attributes at will, and able to show forth attributes higher than mental as it grows, develops and asserts itself on higher planes than the physical and the astral. As I say, the experiments now are very difficult, and training is wanted. The beginning of training along this line of work, which leads us really into what is called the practice of Yoga, is first to use your mind to control your body and your senses, so as to convince yourself that the mind is something higher than the body, more powerful than the senses. Set yourself to work to check some expression of the senses to which you habitually have yielded; cease taking some article of food that is very attractive; drop some form of drink that is very pleasurable and stimulating; leave off some form of physical pleasure to which you are particularly addicted. I do not mean give it up altogether, but give it up for a time, to show that there is something in you, to prove to yourself beyond possibility of dispute that there is something in you that can control all that part of your nature which you call the senses or the bodily expression. Make yourself do a thing against the desire of the senses, and choose a time when the sense is rampant, when it is longing for that particular gratification, eager to have it, when the thing is right in front of you, and you are just putting out your hand to grasp it. Stop and say: "I am stronger than you; you shall not gratify that desire". The only use of the experiment is that it convinces you, as nothing else does, that you are not your senses, and not your body; that you are something higher — let us say for the moment, the mind — and that you can control this body and these senses that very often run away with you. I do not mean that you can always control them; you cannot until you practice; there will be times when the senses, like unbroken horses, will, as it were, take the bit in their teeth and run away with the mind and everything else, and you plunge right after them; they carry you off, but you know even then that they are carrying you off, and you feel that they are stronger than you, and are having their way. In a sort of upside-down fashion, even then you will distinguish between yourself and the wild headlong influences and impulses that hold you captive for the time.

Now, that is a very elementary experiment, but you had better do it so as to be sure there is something in you stronger than the senses. "Oh", you say, "yes, that is the mind. Of course I know my thoughts are above the senses; of course I know that my mind can control my body". All right, keep on doing it, and practice until the body is no obstacle at all; until you can starve all day long and be perfectly good- tempered, even to the last moment; until you can be very tired and exhausted by physical labor and be as bright and even-tempered and sweet-natured to a troublesome child as if you were as fresh as possible. That is what is meant by controlling the body. Keep on practicing until you can do it. It is not much. Keep on doing it until you realize that your body is only your servant, or slave, acting or not acting as you like, and feel the sense of shame when the body is able to make you do what the mind condemns; feel that to do that is to be less than man, less than really human. Dogs snap when they are hungry or angry; human beings ought to be able to be self-controlled; and it is not much to ask that the man shall have control, which only means, after all, that his mind is the master of his body.

So far, then, we shall all agree. Let us suppose that you are now ready to take the next step. That mind of yours is a troublesome thing, after all. It is able to control the body; it is able to control the senses. Is it able to control itself? You find it runs all over the place. You take up a very difficult book and you want to master that book. A good deal depends on your mastering it. Perhaps you are going to pass an examination. Unless you can master that book in the night-time, you will fail, and that will throw you back in your career; so you sit down and work at it; but your mind wanders; when you want to concentrate on some mathematical problem, you are thinking, you find, of something quite different; your mind goes off and you have to bring it back; and this happens over and over again, and you put your book down and you say: "Oh, I am not in the humor; I cannot do it". What sort of a mind is that? It won't work when it is wanted, and it can't do what is its special business, because it is not in the humor. And then you begin to say: "Why shouldn't I control the mind?" And in that very phrase you are asserting something that is higher than the mind — I. "I mean that this mind shall do what I want it to do, and shall be fixed on that book". You concentrate your attention; you gather up something which is strong in you, and you fix the mind on that subject and you work at it. What is it that has done it? It can't be the mind that has done it, which has been running all over the place. It is something that is there which is able to master the mind, and train it to that point where it is wanted to work. Then you feel: "That is the thing I am going to look for now. I have found that the mind is above the senses — I know that; but here is something which is above the mind, and I must go in search of that. Perhaps that is the soul. This force that I feel, which masters my vagrant mind, this strength that I find within myself, which groups my wandering thoughts and compels their obedience, what is that? That seems to be myself. I am controlling my mind". When that point is reached, and when the habit has been formed, so that the mind can be fixed on a thing at order, there will have grown up a definite consciousness of a something which is behind that mind and masters it, as the mind did the senses, and then the student may think it worth while to take steps to find out what that something is. Generally he will have to ask somebody who has gone a little further in this than he has: "What is the next step that I ought to take? I find something here which is higher than, more than, the mind. How am I to find out what it is?" And in some book that he reads, or from some one whom he meets who can explain it to him, he learns that there exist certain practices, definite practices — what are called meditation — by following out which one can develop that consciousness which is higher than the mind.

When a person has reached this point, if no other person comes in his way, you may be sure that he will find a book; he will take up the book in the public library and read it; or some friend will say: "Have you seen that book?" and will introduce the book to him. Somehow or other the book will come in his way. Why? Because there are always more advanced souls watching to see when any evolving soul reaches the point where it can take help, where it is ready for further help; and if there is not available some one in the physical body who can give the help that that soul wants, then it will be directed to the finding of the book where the practical teaching will be given. It is the action of the helpers of men, who come with a helping hand to that seeking soul and place within its reach the knowledge that is the next step in its experiments, and rules for meditation will be found, studied and practiced, and when those rules are studied and practiced what happens is this: That with each day's meditation, the consciousness beyond the mind grows stronger and stronger, more and more able to assert itself, more and more, as it were, revealing itself, until presently the whole center of consciousness will be shifted upwards, and the man will realize that he is not at all his mind, but a great deal more than the mind, and he will then begin to sense things that the mind cannot sense, become conscious of thoughts that the mind is unable to appreciate; and now and then there will come down a great rush, as it were, of thoughts that dominate the mind and that the mind is unable to explain, although it realizes them as true when once they are presented to it. And then arises the question: "I did not argue myself up to this; I did not reach it by logic; I did not reach it by argument; I did not reach it by thinking. It came to me suddenly. Whence did it come?" And the consciousness arises slowly: "It came from myself; that higher part of myself which is beyond the mind, and which in the quiet of the mind is able to assert itself". For, as has often been said, just as a lake unruffled by the wind will reflect sun, or mountain, or flowers, but ruffled gives only broken images; so when the mind is quiet the higher thought is reflected in the lake of the mind, but as long as the winds of thought blow over it, it is ruffled, and only broken images are seen.

In the quiet of the mind, then, the higher thought asserts itself.

Then comes another stage, a higher stage. The student tries more and more to identify himself with the higher thought; gropes after it, as it were; tries to feel it as himself; concentrates his efforts and keeps the mind absolutely still; and at some moment of that experience, without warning, without effort, without anything in which the lower mind takes part, suddenly the consciousness will be outside the body, and the man will know himself as the living consciousness looking at the body that he has left. Over and over again in different Scriptures this statement is found. You may read, for instance, in one of the Hindu Scriptures, that a man should be able to separate the soul from the body as you may separate grass from the sheath that enfolds it. Or, in another phrase, that when the man has dominated the mind, he rises out of the body in a brilliant body of light — a statement literally true. The body in which the soul arises is luminous, radiant, glorious exceedingly — a body of light. No words could better explain this appearance, no phrase more graphically describe the man rising out of the physical body in the astral or in some higher body.

I quote that ancient Scripture in order that you may not for a moment imagine this is simply a modern investigation. All those who know the soul have passed through that experience. It is the final proof that the man is a living soul; not argument, not reasoning, not inference, not authority, not faith, not hearsay, but —

knowledge. "I am this living consciousness, and that body I have left is only a garment that I wore. It is not I; it is not myself. That is not I, I am here; that I have thrown off; I have, escaped from it; I am free from it". And that experience mentioned in those ancient Scriptures is mentioned in other Scriptures, too it is the invariable experience of the prophet, and the teacher, and the seer, for none can truly teach the things of the soul, except by his own knowledge. So long as he is only repeating what intellectually he has learned, he may do a most useful work, but he has not that stamp of first-hand knowledge which carries conviction with it to those whom he teaches. Second-hand knowledge is always liable to be challenged. Questions may be asked which it is almost impossible to answer, if you are only repeating what you have learned intellectually. A necessary stage; I am not speaking against it. All go through it who reach the other. But if the world is still to have witnesses of the immortality of the soul; if the world of the nineteenth century is to have what the world has had in all other ages, the first-hand testimony of living souls that they know that they exist; then men in the nineteenth century must go through the same training that they have gone through in other times, for only thus is first-hand knowledge attainable, and the question of the existence of the soul is put for evermore beyond possibility of doubt or of challenge.

The first time, there may be a sense of bewilderment, or confusion, or wondering what this strange thing is that has happened; but as it is repeated day after day, week after week, month after month, year after year, that consciousness outside the body becomes real — far more real than that within the body; for, coming back into the body time after time, the soul experiences that entering the body is like going into a prison-house; that it is like leaving the open air and going into a cellar or a vault; that the sight is dimmed; that the hearing has grown almost deaf; that all the powers of the soul are limited and deadened, and that this body is indeed as S. Paul, the great Initiate, called it, the body of death, not the body of life.

We call *this* life; it is not life at all. We call it life; it is simply the limited, imprisoned, dull, dwarfed existence which the soul endures for a short time of its experience in order to gain certain physical knowledge which otherwise it would be unable to acquire for lack of suitable instruments. But as you become men of meditation, that higher life becomes your vivid, real life and *this* life becomes a sort of dream, recognized as an illusion, as duties that have to be discharged, obligations that have to be paid, where much has to be done; but the world is a world of prison, of death - not the world of freedom, of life; and then we realize that we, ourselves, are that living, active, powerful, perceiving intelligence to whom the worlds lie open, for whom heaven is the native land, the natural and rightful dwelling-place.

These are the lines along which we pass to the final proof of the existence of the soul. See how gradual the stages have been; how we began on the physical plane with physical experiments; how we passed on then a little into the region of dreams, and action outside the body; how then we took up the question that we recognize by use the difference between the body, and the senses, and the mind; and then how we found the assertion of something beyond that mind more real and more powerful than itself; and then how, encouraged by those lower experiments, we penetrated into the higher, and paid the price which is necessary for that first-hand knowledge of the soul.

Truly, it is worth while. I do not pretend that it can be gained without paying the price. I do not pretend that you can enjoy vehemently the life of the body and the senses and the mind, and at the same time carry on this evolution of the higher life; but this I tell you, that all that you lose is merely the pleasure which you have outgrown, which therefore no longer attracts you. You lose that in the way that you lose your toys when you grow out of childhood; you do not want them. It is not that anyone takes them away from you or breaks them; you do not want them any longer; you have found a higher enjoyment, toys of a finer kind. But the mind is also a toy, though finer than the toy of the senses; that also is recognized as a toy in the higher regions of the life. Gradually then, you give up those pleasures; they have lost their savor; but you perform your duties better than you have performed them before. Don't fall into the mistake that some people do when they begin meditating, of going about the world in their waking life in a fog, in a dream, abstracted, so that everybody says: "Why, that person is losing his mind!" That is not the way to meditate. Meditation makes men more effective, not less keen, not blinder: more alert, not less alert, less observant. The stage wherein people are dreaming is a very early stage of the training of the mind, when they are still so weak that they cannot manage their mind at all; and I have noticed over and over again, if I take for a moment a personal illustration, that I, who have done a good deal in this way of meditation, who have trained myself carefully along the road that I have been pointing out to you, I often notice when I am with people who have never dreamed of this at all, and who call themselves quick, observant people of the world, that I see things that they miss, observe things that pass them unobserved, notice all kinds of tiny things in the streets, in the railway cars, in people, which pass by them without making the slightest impression. And I only mention that to show you that it is not necessary to lose the powers of the lower mind, while you are busy evolving the higher. The fact is, you have them much more at your command, and just because you do not wear them out by worry, and fuss, and anxiety, they are much more available when you want to use them; indeed, common sense is very marked, and reason, logic, intelligence, caution, prudence, all these qualities come out strongly and brilliantly in the true Occultist.

The man becomes greater and not less on the mental plane, because he works in a region beyond and above the intellect. He has gained in life. He is not robbed of the lower life; he has lost it, and in losing it he finds it. Resigning the lower, he finds the higher flowing into him fully, and the lower is more brilliant than it ever was before. He asks for nothing: everything comes to him. He seeks for nothing; all things flow to him unasked. He makes no demands; nature pours out on him her treasures. He is ever pouring forth all that he possesses. He is always full, though ever emptying himself.

Those are the paradoxes of the life of the soul; those the realities proven as true, when the existence of the soul is known, and if tonight I have not tried to win you by mere skill of tongue or picture, or what would be called appeals to emotion and feelings, it is because I wanted to win your reason step by step along this path; because I wanted to show you — without emotion, without appeals to intuition, without making, as I might make, appeal to that knowledge within every one of you — that you are immortal existences and that death is not your master. Instead of appealing to that, as I have the right to appeal to it, I have led you step by step along the path of the reason; I have shown you why you should take each new step when the others behind are taken. But let me, in concluding, say a word to those who do not need to take the lower steps of this toilsome path, who do not need to prove that the soul exists, who are filled with the consciousness that they are living souls, who, though they know it not first hand, by knowledge, yet have a deep, undying conviction that no logic can shake, no argument can alter, no scoff can vary, no jeer and no proof can change. Beaten in argument, confused by logic, bewildered by proof, they still say: "I feel, I know, I am a living soul". To those I would say: trouble not yourselves about the lower steps; trouble not yourselves with all the arguments I was using as proof over and over again reiterated, intended to convince the materialist. Trust your intuition, and act on its truth. The inner voice never misleads. It is the Self whispering of its own existence and imperially commanding your belief. Yield your belief to the voice within. Take it for true, though you have not proved it as true, and act on that internal conviction as though it were true. Then begin the processes of meditation to which I hastily alluded. Take, as you may take, the books where these are traced out for you one by one. Begin to practice them. Do not waste any more time in reasoning out other processes that you are not ready to understand. Trust the voice within you. Follow the guidance which has been marked out for you by those who have trodden that road and have proved it to be true. Then swiftly and easily you will gain the knowledge. Then, without long delay, you will know of your own knowledge that these things are true. If the soul speaks to you, don't wait for the confirmation of the intellect. Trust the divine voice; obey the divine impulse; follow out the road traced by sages, by prophets, by teachers, verified by disciples who, in the present day, have trodden it, and know it to lead to the rightful goal. Then you, too, shall know; then you, too, shall share; then your intuition shall be confirmed by knowledge, and you shall feel yourselves the living, the immortal soul. That is my message to you then, to those who need not the proof, and appeal to the intuition; and in giving you the message, I speak not of myself; in giving you the message, I bring you no new thing; I confirm to you in your own day and time, what every prophet has asserted, what every disciple has taught, what every divine man has proclaimed. As a messenger of that Brotherhood, I do but repeat Their message.

There is the weight of the evidence, and not in my poor reassertion of it. What is it that one soul should have found to be true, that which all the great souls have declared? If you would have authority, take it on their word. Remember that what I speak is indeed spoken with my lips, but with Their voice; I bring to you the testimony of the ages; I bring to you the message from an innumerable company. I, but weak and poor in my own knowledge, limited and circumscribed in my own experience, servant of that great Brotherhood, holding it the proudest privilege and delight to be able to serve and to give my obedience, I speak Their word. I do not dare to endorse it, as it were, though knowing it to be true. I put it on Their testimony, unshakable, immovable, back to the furthest antiquity, down to the present day, an unbroken army of mighty witnesses, an innumerable company of prophets, of teachers, of saints. Their messenger, I speak Their message. You can prove its truth for yourselves, if you will.

Other Books in this Series and Related Titles

Theosophical Basics by William Q Judge (978–1–63118–608–0)

The Hebrew Talisman by Richard Harte (978–1–63118–607–3)

Early Masonic Symbolism by Manly P Hall (978–1–63118–606–6)

Nature Spirits and Elementals by Louise Off (978-1-63118-605-9)

Swedenborg Bifrons by H P Blavatsky (978-1-63118-604-2)

Practical Use of Psychic Powers by C W Leadbeater (978-1-63118-603-5)

Using White & Black Magic by C W Leadbeater (978-1-63118-602-8)

Jesus, the Last Great Initiate by Edouard Schure (978-1-63118-599-1)

Mysterious Wonders of Antiquity by Manly P Hall (978-1-63118-598-4)

Ancient Mysteries and Secret Societies by Manly P Hall (978–1–63118–597–7)

The Zodiac and Its Signs by Manly P Hall (978–1–63118–596–0)

Life and Teachings of Hermes Trismegistus by Manly P Hall (978–1–63118–595–3)

The Secrets of Doctor Taverner by Dion Fortune (978–1–63118–594–6)

Vegetarianism, Theosophy & Occultism by Leadbeater &c (978–1–63118–593–9)

Applied Theosophy by Henry S Olcott (978–1–63118–592–2)

Higher Consciousness by C W Leadbeater (978–1–63118–591–5)

Theories About Reincarnation and Spirits by H P Blavatsky (978–1–63118–590–8)

The Use and Power of Thought by C W Leadbeater (978–1–63118–589–2)

Commentary on the Pymander by G R S Mead (978–1–63118–588–5)

Hypnotism and Mesmerism by Annie Besant (978–1–63118–587–8)

Spirits of Various Kinds by Helena P Blavatsky (978–1–63118–586–1)

The Hidden Language of Symbolism by Annie Besant (978–1–63118–585–4)

Eastern Magic & Western Spiritualism by Henry S Olcott (978–1–63118–584–7)

Spiritual Progress and Practical Occultism by H P Blavatsky (978–1–63118–583–0)

Memory and Consciousness by Besant & Blavatsky (978–1–63118–582–3)

The Origin of Evil by Helena P Blavatsky (978–1–63118–581–6)

The Camp of Philosophy: Studies in Alchemy by Bloomfield (978–1–63118–580–9)

The Testaments of the Twelve Patriarchs (978–1–63118–579–3)

Occult or Exact Science? by Helena P Blavatsky (978–1–63118–578–6)

Occultism, Semi-Occultism & Pseudo Occultism by A Besant (978–1–63118–577–9)

The Fourth-Gospel and Synoptical Problem by G R S Mead (978–1–63118–576–2)

On the Bhagavad-Gita by T Subba Row &c (978–1–63118–575–5)

What Theosophy Does for Us by C W Leadbeater (978–1–63118–574–8)

Spiritual Life for Man by Annie Besant (978–1–63118–573–1)

The Mysteries by Annie Besant (978–1–63118–572–4)

Fundamental Ideas of Theosophy by Bhagwan Das (978–1–63118–571–7)

Dreams: What They Are and How They Are Caused (978–1–63118–570–0)

Communication Between Different Worlds by Annie Besant (978–1–63118–569–4)

Animism, Magic and the Omnipotence of Thought by S Freud (978–1–63118–568–7)

Buddhism by F Otto Schrader (978–1–63118–567–0)

Death by W W Westcott (978–1–63118–566–3)

The Religion of Theosophy by Bhagwan Das (978–1–63118–565–6)

The Spirit of Zoroastrianism by Henry S Olcott (978–1–63118–564–9)

The Brotherhood of Religions by Annie Besant (978–1–63118–563–2)

Fourth Book of Maccabees by Josephus (978-1-63118-562-5)

The Story of Ahikar by Ahiqar (978-1-63118-561-8)

Vision of the Spirit by C. Jinarajadasa (978-1-63118-560-1)

Occult Arts by William Q. Judge (978-1-63118-559-5)

Kali the Mother by Sister Nivedita (978-1-63118-558-8)

Love and Death by Sri Aurobindo (978–1–63118–557–1)

Times and Seasons Volume 1, Numbers 4-6 (978-1-63118-556-4)

Times and Seasons Volume 1, Numbers 1-3 (978-1-63118-555-7)

The Book of John Whitmer by John Whitmer (978-1-63118-554-0)

Interesting Account of Several Remarkable Visions (978-1-63118-553-3)

The Evening and Morning Star Volume 1, Numbers 11 & 12 (978-1-63118-552-6)

The Evening and Morning Star Volume 1, Numbers 1 & 2 (978-1-63118-547-2)

Private Diary of Joseph Smith 1832-1834 (978-1-63118-546-5)

An Address to All Believers in Christ Elder David Whitmer (978-1-63118-545-8)

A Manuscript on Far West by Reed Peck (978-1-63118-544-1)

The Story of Mormonism by James E Talmage (978-1-63118-543-4)

The Philosophy of Mormonism by James E Talmage (978-1-63118-542-7)

The Angel of the Prairies or A Dream of the Future (978-1-63118-541-0)

The Book of Abraham: Mormon History by George Reynolds (978-1-63118-540-3)

Pearl of Great Price by Joseph Smith (978-1-63118-539-7)

Taittiriya Upanishad and Commentary by Charles Johnston (978-1-63118-538-0)

Initiation and the Great Mysteries by C H Vail (978-1-63118-537-3)

Yoga Sutras of Patanjali and Commentary by Charles Johnston (978-1-63118-536-6)

Essays on Ancient Magic by Helena P Blavatsky (978-1-63118-535-9)

The Hidden Mysteries of Christianity by Annie Besant (978-1-63118-534-2)

The Historic, Mythic and Mystic Christ by Annie Besant (978-1-63118-533-5)

The Use of Evil by Annie Besant (978-1-63118-532-8)

The Inmost Light and Other Tales by Arthur Machen (978-1-63118-531-1)

The Eleusinian Mysteries by Dudley Wright (978-1-63118-530-4)

The Wendigo and Other Haunting Tales Algernon Blackwood (978-1-63118-529-8)

The Great God Pan by Arthur Machen (978-1-63118-528-1)

The Apocalypse of Peter by Peter (978-1-63118-527-4)

The Vision of Saint Paul the Apostle by Paul (978-1-63118-526-7)

The Comte de St. Germain: the Secret of Kings Cooper-Oakley (978-1-63118-525-0)

The Golden Chain of Homer by Anton Josef Kirchweger (978-1-63118-524-3)

With the Adepts or an Adventure Among the Rosicrucians (978-1-63118-523-6)

The Treasure of Atlantis by J Allan Dunn (978-1-63118-522-9)

Early Translation of the Acts of the Apostles by Luke (978-1-63118-521-2)

Book of Vexations by Paracelsus (978-1-63118-520-5)

Hermetic Arcanum by Jean d'Espagnet (978-1-63118-519-9)

A Weird Tale and Other Supernatural Stories by W Q Judge (978-1-63118-518-2)

The Secret Book of the Philosopher's Stone by Artephius (978-1-63118-517-5)

Initiation of the Great Pyramid by Manly P Hall (978-1-63118-516-8)

The A. E. Waite Reader: A Selection of Occult Essays (978-1-63118-515-1)

Freher's Process in the Philosophical Work by D A Freher (978-1-63118-514-4)

The Alchemical Catechism of Paracelsus by Paracelsus (978-1-63118-513-7)

The Life of Pythagoras by Porphyry (978-1-63118-512-0)

On the Philadelphian Gold by Philochrysus & Philadelphus (978-1-63118-511-3)

A Collection of Fiction and Essays by Occult Writers on Supernatural and Metaphysical Subjects by various (978-1-63118-510-6)

The Stone of the Philosophers by A E Waite (978-1-63118-509-0)

Freemasonry & Catholicism by Max Heindel (978-1-63118-508-3)

Aurora of the Philosophers by Paracelsus (978-1-63118-507-6)

Brothers and Builders by Joseph Fort Newton (978-1-63118-506-9)

On the Cave of the Nymphs in the Odyssey by Porphyry (978-1-63118-505-2)

The Symbols and Legends of Masonry by C H Vail (978-1-63118-504-5)

The Odes of Solomon by King Solomon (978-1-63118-503-8)

The Book of Wisdom of Solomon by King Solomon (978-1-63118-502-1)

The Sword of Welleran and Other Stories by Lord Dunsany (978-1-63118-501-4)

The Magician's Heavenly Chaos by Thomas Vaughan (978-1-63118-500-7)

The Devil in Love by Jacques Cazotte (978-1-63118-499-4)

Atlantis, the Gods of Antiquity and the Myth of the Dying God (978-1-63118-498-7)

Mandukya Upanishad and Commentary by Charles Johnston (978-1-63118-497-0)

Mundaka Upanishad and Commentary by Charles Johnston (978-1-63118-496-3)

Tao Te Ching & Commentary by Lao Tzu & C Johnston (978-1-63118-495-6)

Prashna Upanishad and Commentary by Charles Johnston (978-1-63118-494-9)

Katha Upanishad and Commentary by Charles Johnston (978-1-63118-493-2)

The Hymn of Jesus by G. R. S. Mead (978-1-63118-492-5)

Kena Upanishad and Commentary by Charles Johnston (978-1-63118-491-8)

Isha Upanishad and Commentary by Charles Johnston (978-1-63118-490-1)

Audio versions are also available on Audible, Amazon and Apple

www.ingramcontent.com/pod-product-compliance
Lightning Source LLC
LaVergne TN
LVHW050947080826
845145LV00004B/1445

* 9 7 8 1 6 3 1 1 8 6 3 8 7 *